Living Legends

...Six Stories about Successful Deaf People

by
Darlene Toole

Butte Publications, Inc.
Hillsboro, Oregon

Living Legends

Acknowledgments:
Pictures: provided by the subjects, used
          by permission.
Reviewers: Jim and Dorothy McCarr
Editor: Ellen Todras
Designer: Anita Jones

Note: A percentage of the proceeds will be donated to Infant Hearing Resource (IHR), a department of the Hearing and Speech Institute (HSI) located in Portland, Oregon. IHR serves deaf and hard-of-hearing children ages infancy to four and their families. All forms of communication are encouraged.

Butte Publications, Inc.
P.O. Box 1328
Hillsboro, OR 97123-1328
U.S.A.

ISBN: 1-884362-13-3

Table of Contents

Dedication: To my son, Eric, with love.

"The future belongs to those who believe in the beauty of their dreams."

ELEANOR ROOSEVELT

Introduction
(To the Teacher)

Living Legends is a book of six stories about deaf people who have displayed courageous effort in achieving excellence in their chosen vocations or avocations.

At the beginning of each story, there is a word list with simple definitions to help students understand some vocabulary words that will be used in the story.

At the end of each story are comprehension questions.

These questions can be used to test the students' understanding individually or as a group.

One creative writing exercise also follows each story. Encourage students to create their own paragraphs or stories to help develop their writing skills.

How To Use This Book

This book contains six stories. Each story has a vocabulary introduction page and two different exercises.

Words to Know - Vocabulary Introduction Page
Before each story there are vocabulary words with simple definitions. Study these words before you read the story. Discuss these words with your teacher.

Stories
Read each story carefully. Check the words you do not know on the vocabulary introduction page.

Check Your Understanding Exercise
At the end of each story there are some comprehension questions that will help you remember what you read. Discuss your answers with your teacher and classmates.

Write About Exercise
This exercise will help you develop better writing skills. Share your paragraphs and stories with your teacher and classmates.

Evelyn Glennie:
Words to Know

musician
a person who expresses him/ herself through a musical instrument

instruments
things or devices used to make musical sounds.

Examples:drums, bells, rattles, xylophones

Grammy Award
a special music award

Scotland
an area in the northern part of Great Britian

tomboy
a girl who likes to do activities that are generally thought of as boys' activities

talent
skill: ability

concert
a musical performance

to encourage
to give hope

to discover
to find out

gradual
steady

mystery	something that cannot be explained
to overcome	to beat: to conquer
percussionist	a musician who plays the drums, cymbols, xylophone, etc.
perfect pitch	the talent of being able to recognize an exact pitch
academy	a school or place of specialized training
to amaze	to surprise
mentor	a wise adviser
solo	an activity performed by one person
to perform	to do: to act
orchestra	a group of musicians playing together

Evelyn Glennie:
The Impossible Dream

Photo by: Harrison/Parrott Ltd.

Have you ever met a deaf **musician**? Have you ever met someone who can play over 600 **instruments**? Have you ever met a deaf person who has won a **Grammy Award**? If not, it is time to meet Evelyn Glennie.

Evelyn Glennie was born in 1965 on a farm in northeast **Scotland**. She was a beautiful **tomboy** who loved to play outdoors with her friends and two older brothers. Her family was very close and she had a wonderful childhood.

The Glennie family enjoyed Scottish traditional music, and young Evelyn showed great musical

talent. As a child, Evelyn's favorite instruments were a toy guitar, clarinet, and piano. She begged and begged her parents for music lessons and once she got them, she practiced daily.

When she was eight years old, Evelyn waited her turn to play the piano at a small **concert**. Someone called her name, but she did not move. She did not hear her name. Evelyn was becoming deaf!

For many months, Evelyn's ears ached and felt so sore that she did not want to play outside. She was having problems in school because she could not hear her teachers and classmates. Evelyn was very smart and she tried to hide her deafness from others, but the principal of her school finally **encouraged** her parents to take Evelyn to see a doctor.

The doctor **discovered** that Evelyn had **gradual** nerve damage in both ears. He could not explain why. It was a **mystery**. He told her she needed powerful hearing aids and suggested she attend a school for deaf children.

Evelyn's parents were heartbroken. Her mother sadly exclaimed, "It was like a slap in the face. Everything **suddenly looked black**."

Evelyn did not want to leave her family and friends, so she decided not to attend a school for deaf children. She decided to wear hearing aids, but she grew her hair long to cover her ears. She also taught herself to lipread. Evelyn's friends took notes for her in class, and she struggled to **overcome** her deafness; she never gave up. She said, "Somehow I would cope with my deafness; it was just a matter of getting used to it."

For many years, Evelyn continued to enjoy music and refused to let her deafness stop her. She even dreamed of becoming a concert pianist. Then, when she was 12 years old, she saw a girl playing a xylophone. Evelyn was in awe! This experience changed her life and her dream. From then on, she wanted to become a **percussionist**. Percussionists play instruments such as the xylophone, drums, cymbals, and tambourine.

Many teachers discouraged Evelyn from being a percussionist. Some thought it was an impossible dream, but Evelyn was stubborn and determined. Luckily, she had "**perfect pitch**" and the special skill "to feel" music from her heart to her toes. She explains, "Music pours through every part of my body. It tingles in my skin, my cheekbones, even my hair."

When Evelyn was 16 years old, she decided to make music her life. She attended the famous Royal **Academy** of Music in London, England. She was the first deaf person to try out, and she scored one of the highest marks in the history of the Academy. Evelyn Glennie **amazed** everyone. Her dear friend and **mentor**, James Blades, a famous percussionist, said, "She will make history!"

Evelyn is now a **solo** percussionist known all over the world. Some people think that playing percussion instruments is hitting, banging, and clanging. Evelyn proves with all of her heart that it is much more. It is an experience that can make you laugh and cry. It can make you feel alive!

Believe it or not, Evelyn plays over 600

instruments. Her favorite hobby is collecting instruments from her travels. She continues to **perform** all over the world in concerts with famous **orchestras**. She has appeared on television and has made many recordings. In 1989, she wrote her life story, called *Good Vibrations*.

Photo by: Carol Weinberg/BMG

Evelyn Glennie has made history in the music world. This award-winning musician has given people great pleasure with her beautiful music. She says with her large brown eyes and lovely smile, "My deafness is something special and I treasure it, and I don't want it taken away. I want to stay as I am. Sometimes my deafness has even helped me."

Check Your Understanding

1. How did Evelyn's mother feel when she found out that Evelyn was becoming deaf?

2. What information from the story tells you that Evelyn had great musical talent as a child?

3. What experience changed Evelyn's life when she was 12 years old?

4. How do you know that Evelyn is a successful musician?

5. What do you think would have happened to Evelyn if she had not become deaf?

6. Why do you think Ms. Glennie treasures her deafness?

Write About

Evelyn Glennie can play over 600 musical instruments. If you could choose to play a musical instrument, which would you pick? Explain why.

Howie Seago:
Words to Know

producer   a person who makes or creates something

performer   a person who acts or entertains

hereditary   passed on from an ancestor or relative

forbidden   not allowed

to enroll   to become a member; to join

psychology   the study of the mind and the way people and animals behave

to pantomime   to tell a story, using gestures, body movements, and facial expressions without talking

to memorize   to learn by heart: to remember

to tour   to travel

NTD   The **N**ational **T**heatre of the **D**eaf began in 1967. It is a professional theatre company of deaf and hearing actors who use both signs and spoken language.

valuable   worthy; having importance

character	a person in a book, play, story, or movie
popular	well-liked; admired
to create	to make
science fiction	an imaginative story about science
to impress	to have a strong effect
expression	showing thoughts and feelings
to respect	to show honor
senior citizen	an elderly adult over the age of 65
volunteers	people who offer to help without getting paid
trailblazer	a person who is first to try to do something

Howie Seago: The Trailblazer

Howie Seago is a man for all seasons. He is an actor, **producer**, director, teacher, and writer. This talented **performer** grew up in Tacoma, Washington. He comes from a large family of seven. His father and two brothers are deaf, while his mother and two sisters are hearing. Howie explains, "Deafness is **hereditary** in my family, but my parents did a great job raising us. Children do well if they have love. That's why I'm where I am today."

Deaf since birth, Howie grew up in an oral program for deaf children that supported speech and lipreading. Sign language was **forbidden**. From an early age, Howie wanted to communicate with his hands to express himself, so he and his deaf brothers, David and Billy, used homemade signs. Later, Howie attended mainstreamed classes in Tacoma Public Schools. He shared some classes with other deaf students and also went to some classes with hearing students.

After graduation from high school, Howie **enrolled** at California State University, Northridge, (CSUN). A whole new world opened up for him there. At CSUN, he met many deaf people from different backgrounds and learned American Sign Language (ASL). He also grew as a person because of these experiences and new challenges.

At CSUN, Howie majored in **psychology** and theatre arts. The acting bug first bit him in junior high school, not college. His family was active in a local church where his mother directed plays. She chose Howie to be in one of the church plays, and he **pantomimed** the leading character while a hearing person voiced for him. People who watched young Howie knew he had talent and would be successful as an actor.

Howie enjoyed the thrill of performing. Yet, he did not act again until college at CSUN. There, his college roommate was planning to direct a play and asked Howie to be in it. He was worried because his sign language ability was limited, but he worked hard and **memorized** his lines. Since then, he has been involved in the theatre.

During the past 25 years, Howie Seago has acted in, produced, and directed many different plays around the United States and the world. For several years, he **toured** with the **National Theatre of the Deaf (NTD)**. This famous group of deaf and hearing actors performs in both ASL and spoken English. Howie starred in many plays with the NTD and gained **valuable** experience in the theatre.

Howie Seago is one person, but he has been many different **characters** on the stage: Ajax, Orin, Achilles, Enkidu, and The Beast, to name a few! He has won several awards for his outstanding acting ability.

Photo by : Ruthalz Fotografin

Howie is not only a stage actor, he has also acted on **popular** television shows. The most exciting television role Howie got was in "Star Trek: The Next Generation." He was encouraged by his wife, Lori, to **create** a role for himself in his favorite **science fiction** show. Howie presented ideas for how a deaf character could communicate and **impressed** the producer of the show with his creativity. Thousands of people watched Howie as Riva and loved his performance. He has also performed on these television shows: "The Equalizer," "Hunter," and "Rainbow's End."

Howie currently lives in Seattle with his wife and two sons. He teaches creative uses of ASL at Seattle Central Community College. He is also the director of a special deaf youth drama program at Seattle Children's Theatre. Somehow Howie and his brother Billy have found time to create a series of entertaining video stories for children called Visual Tales.

Howie feels strongly about deaf actors and deaf people in general. He feels that deaf actors can be just as good as anybody else, and that deaf people need to use their power of sign language to develop storytelling and **expression**. He feels strongly that hearing and deaf people must **respect** individual differences. He says, "People should accept the deaf person for whoever they are, whether they can speak with their voice or not. What I am happy to do as a deaf adult is give the deaf child and person a glow inside of themselves - a spark to say, Hey, I can do it and I will try my best!'"

Howie continues to produce and direct plays for the Deaf Community. He hopes that deaf artists will get involved and work with deaf children in schools throughout the United States and around the world. He also encourages older deaf people who are retired or **senior citizens** to **volunteer** their time working with deaf youth. This amazing **trailblazer**, Howie Seago, continues to blaze trails for deaf children all over America!

Check Your Understanding

1. In what ways was attending CSUN a good experience?

2. Who encouraged Howie to get a role on "Star Trek?"

3. What are some different kinds of jobs that Mr. Seago has had?

4. Why do you think Howie became an actor?

5. Do you think that Howie is a good role model for young deaf actors and actresses? Explain your answer.

6. Can you tell about one of Howie's future goals?

Write About

Howie Seago had a role on the television show "Star Trek: The Next Generation." What is your favorite television show? Explain why.

Shirley Allen:
Words to Know

coma	unconciousness due to illness or injury
to influence	to have a strong effect on someone
career	the work a person does through life
to transfer	to move from one place to another
independent	depending on self
clerk	a person who works in an office
Gallaudet University	the only accredited liberal arts university for deaf people in the world and is located in Washington, D.C.
supervisor	director
dormitories	a building that has many bedrooms
campus	the grounds and buildings of a school or college
M.A. degree	Masters of Arts Degree

counseling	advising and helping
a challenge	an effort
a professor	a teacher who works at a college or university
NTID	National Technical Institute for the Deaf is located in Rochester, New York
technical	special skills in mechanical and industrial arts
professional	trained and educated
eager	enthusiastic
Ph.D.	Doctor of Philosophy
courage	bravery
culture	the arts, beliefs, customs that make up a way of life for a group of people

Shirley Allen:
Follow Every Rainbow

"Music was always my first love," says Shirley Allen. Shirley loved to sing and play the piano. She studied music in college. Her dream was to become a concert pianist or blues singer/pianist.

Everything changed when she was 20 years old. She became sick with what doctors think was typhoid fever. This terrible illness caused her to have a high fever and rash. Shirley was in a **coma** for five weeks and she almost died. Doctors gave her medicine to help her get well, but the medicine caused her to become totally deaf. Shirley never heard again.

She could no longer hear the music which she had always loved.

Shirley Jeanne Allen was born in Texas. Her parents divorced when she was a young girl, and she moved around and lived with different family members. She lived with her mother, grandmother, aunts, cousins, great aunts, and her father and stepmother, with whom she lived the longest. "My grandmother had the biggest **influence** on me," says Shirley, "but the longest I ever lived with anyone was eight years."

Living with so many different people was not always easy, yet it was not a bad experience. Shirley learned to get along with different kinds of people. She learned to understand people's moods and personalities. This experience helped her become wise and mature.

After graduating from high school, Shirley attended Talladega College in Alabama. Then she transferred to Jarvis Christian College in Texas. She majored in music, but it was during her junior year that she lost her hearing. She continued to play the piano and even returned to college after her illness to give a piano concert!

Shirley would never give up playing the piano, but she did decide to change **careers**. She said, "Instead of becoming a deaf concert pianist, I decided to try something else." She **transferred** to Gallaudet University and studied English. In 1966, Shirley graduated from Gallaudet and looked for a job. She wanted to be **independent** and work full-time.

For three years, Shirley worked as a **clerk** in

Washington, D.C. Then, in 1967 she was asked to work at **Gallaudet University** as a dorm **supervisor**. Most college students at Gallaudet live in **dormitories**. Shirley supervised young women who lived on **campus** during the school year. She also taught English. Somehow she found time to attend graduate school at Howard University in Washington, D.C. In 1972, Shirley received her **M.A. degree** in **counseling**.

Always ready for a new **challenge**, Shirley became a **professor** at **National Technical Institute for the Deaf (NTID)** in 1973. NTID is located in Rochester, New York. This college offers deaf and hard-of-hearing students **technical** and **professional** training.

When Shirley started teaching at NTID, she was young and **eager**. She was also the only black and deaf teacher on campus. Shirley says with a smile, "When the students saw me walk into the classroom for the first time, they looked as if they had seen a ghost! Many of them had never seen a non-white teacher before." Shirley, who comes from a family teachers, has taught at NTID for over 22 years!

This amazing woman became the first black deaf female in the world to receive her **Ph.D.** She made history in 1992, when she received the highest degree in education from the University of Rochester in New York. Her very proud 92-year-old grandmother attended the graduation and cheered her on.

Dr. Shirley Jeanne Allen has traveled many roads and followed many rainbows searching for her dream. With **courage** and determination, she never gave up. Shirley sums up her goal in life: "I want to do everything possible to help make the world a better place in which to live for deaf and hard-of-hearing persons, others with disabilities, and people from differing **cultures**."

Check Your Understanding

1. What might have happened to Shirley if she had not become deaf at the age of 20?

2. Why do you think Shirley changed career plans after she became deaf?

3. Why do you think Dr. Allen became a teacher?

4. What are some different kinds of jobs that Dr. Allen had before she became a professor at NTID?

5. How do you think Shirley felt when she was the only black and deaf teacher on campus at NTID?

6. Where does Shirley live now?

Write About

Dr. Shirley Allen worked very hard to achieve her dream. Write a paragraph about a special goal or dream that you have. Tell why it is important to you.

John Woo:
Words to Know

target   a mark or spot that is aimed at

skydiving   the sport of jumping from an airplane and falling before the parachute opens

Hong Kong   a colony of Great Britian on the southern coast of China. It will become part of China in 1997.

private   1. not public; 2. secret

CSDB   California School for the Deaf, Berkeley; moved to a new campus in Fremont, California, in 1980.

B.A. degree   the first degree of a college or university

computer programmer   a person who writes programs for computers

CADS   Center for Assessment and Demographic Studies at Gallaudet University

data   information such as facts and numbers

to fascinate	to attract; to charm
risky	dangerous
daredevil	a person who performs dangerous stunts
equipment	things needed; supplies
canopy	a covering made of cloth or other material. Example: an open parachute
reserve parachute	the backup parachute jumpers have that is packed by a licensed rigger
a rigger	a person licensed by the FAA to pack reserve parachutes
FAA	Federal Aviation Agency; makes rules for airplane safety
to injure	to hurt
to compete	to try to win
Taiwan	an island country off the eastern coast of China
fencing	the sport of fighting with a sword or a foil

John Woo:
The Divine Dragon

Imagine being in an airplane and jumping out at 10,000 feet in the air. Then suddenly, your parachute opens at 2,500 feet as you sail down, landing on a **target** - a small spot on the ground. John Woo, an expert parachute jumper, thinks that **skydiving** is a perfect sport for deaf people because hearing is not important. He says, "The reason I started skydiving is because I want to make people realize that deaf people can jump and that jumping is a safe sport."

John, who has been deaf since birth, was born in Canton, China, in 1948. He has three brothers and one sister. All of his family is hearing except for him.

Doctors cannot explain why John is deaf, but he can only hear loud noises.

When he was seven years old, his family moved to **Hong Kong**. John attended a **private** oral school for deaf children. He learned Chinese, but sign language was not allowed. John and his friends made up their own signs to communicate in private.

At the age of 14, John's family moved to the United States. They settled in California. John's parents wanted him to get a good education and medical help. He enrolled at the **California School for the Deaf (CSDB)**, which was located in Berkeley, California, at that time.

After graduating from high school, John attended Gallaudet University in Washington, D.C. At Gallaudet, he majored in math and received his **B.A. degree** in 1974. He enjoyed working with computers and decided to stay at Gallaudet to work as a **computer programmer**.

John has worked at Gallaudet's **Center for Assessment and Demographic Studies (CADS)** for 20 years. At CADS, Mr. Woo collects numbers and other information about deaf and hard-of-hearing children in the United States. He gathers the info or **data** and programs it into his computer. He shares the information with his research team, and it helps them understand the needs of deaf children in this country.

How did John become interested in parachute jumping? John first became **fascinated** with jumping when he was a young boy and watched the popular television show "The Ripcord." This TV series was about parachute jumping. For many years, he wanted to try parachute jumping, but people told him it was a **risky** and unsafe sport for deaf people. John says, "In the past, deaf people were not encouraged to do **daredevil** stunts."

Finally, in 1981, John got the opportunity to take a parachute jumping class at Gallaudet. Twelve deaf people signed up for the class, but only John finished! The other people dropped out. The first time John jumped he said, "I was scared and nervous like anybody else. But I have learned that deaf people can jump without any problems."

Students who take a parachute-jumping class learn that there are five important parts:
1. **Equipment** (costs between $2,000 and $3,000)
   a. Clothing
   b. The main parachute
   c. The reserve parachute;
2. Going up in the airplane;
3. Skydiving while jumping;
4. **Canopy** riding while the main parachute is open;
5. Landing.

Parachute jumpers pack their own main parachute, but all jumpers must have a **reserve parachute**. This extra parachute must be packed by "**a rigger**" who has a license from the **Federal Aviation Administration (FAA)**. Riggers make sure the reserve parachute works and keeps the jumper safe. John adds, "I was never **injured** while in the air, but once I sprained my ankle while landing on the ground." For safety reasons, no one can jump without passing a written test first.

Since John's first jump in 1981, he has made over 1,200 jumps. He loves to **compete** in different skydiving events. Sometimes he jumps solo; other times with two or more people.

John was the only deaf member of a skydiving team called "The Divine Dragons." The team traveled and competed in many different places. One of John's best memories was traveling to **Taiwan** with the team, where he won several medals for his outstanding jumps. John is working hard to start a national group of deaf parachute jumpers. He thinks there are about 20 deaf jumpers in the United States.

The first deaf person to become a master parachute jumper was Fred Goebel of Texas. He has made over 1,300 jumps! In 1993, John and Fred helped organize a team of four deaf jumpers called "The Silent Free Fall Team." John says, "My goal is to find eight deaf jumpers so they can join together in the air to set a new world record."

John Woo also competes locally and nationally in **fencing**. When he was 10 years old, a classmate threw a rock and blinded him in the left eye. John says it's "no problem" for him and he has won many ribbons and medals in this sport. His other interests are soccer, snow skiing, photography, and cooking Chinese food.

John loves a challenge. He is a daredevil who believes in himself. He says, "I'm trying to achieve what is best for me and at the same time trying to make people respect and understand deaf people better."

Check Your Understanding

1. When did John and his family move to the United States?

2. What does John do for a living?

3. Describe how John felt when he made his first parachute jump.

4. Why do "riggers" have an important job?

5. Why do you think John Woo thinks parachute jumping is a safe sport?

Write About

John Woo is an outstanding athlete. He parachute jumps, fences, plays soccer, and skis. Write about your favorite sport. Explain why you like this sport.

Karen L. Meyer: Words to Know

correspondent a reporter

issues subjects; topics

disability a barrier to overcome
Examples: deafness, blindness

advocate supporter

capable able

to exclaim to speak with strong feeling

mainstreamed classes attending regular classes in public school with or without support services

Latin the language of ancient Romans

determination a firm purpose

social worker a person who works with people to improve their lives

consultant	a person who helps people by telling them how to help others improve services
ADA	**A**merican with **D**isabilities **A**ct; became a law in 1990
access	the right to use; the right to enter
employment	work
attitudes	a way of feeling toward someone or something
dynamic	active; energetic
]to research	to carefully study and find information
script	written information
to discriminate	to treat some people different from others for unfair reasons
a firm	a company; a business

Karen L. Meyer:
Making Headlines

Karen L. Meyer is the first deaf **correspondent** to report on issues pertaining to people with disabilities in the United States to be on a news program along with hearing reporters. She appears on WLS-TV, the ABC-owned station in Chicago. Karen says, "Every week, I do a report on different **issues** related to **disabilities**." People often call Karen an "**advocate**" of disabled people because she has a personal and professional interest in helping them.

Karen has been deaf since birth, and she knows that disabled workers are **capable**. There are over 49 million Americans who are disabled. Karen proudly **exclaims**, "It is my goal to make the every-day world accessible for 49 million Americans with disabilities."

When Karen was growing up in Wilmette, Illinois, she never dreamed she would become a TV correspondent. Karen and her brother, who also is deaf, attended **mainstreamed classes** without having interpreters. They used their speech and lipreading skills and had to work very hard on their own.

During high school and college, Karen had notetakers, but she still had to spend lots of time reading and studying to make good grades. Her favorite subjects at Evanston Township High School were history and **Latin**.

Karen attended Eastern Illinois University and received her B.A. (Bachelor of Arts) degree in social work in 1976. She learned sign language for the first time when she was 19 years old. Then, she got her M.A. (Master of Arts) degree from Loyola University in Chicago in 1985. At Loyola University, Karen had an interpreter for the first time in her classes. She felt this was a positive experience and very helpful. Because of her hard work and **determination**, Karen was very successful as a col-lege student, and she never let her deafness stop her from achieving her goal to become a social worker.

Since 1976, Karen has been involved with public service. As a **social worker**, she has had many different roles. She has been an advocate, counselor, **consultant**, public speaker, leader, and even a bridge! How can a person be a bridge? Ask Karen and she will tell you, "I'm a bridge for my community because I have lived in both worlds."

During the past 18 years, she has worked very hard to improve the lives, homes, and jobs of many disabled and homeless people not only in Chicago, but throughout the United States. She has also traveled across the country, speaking and helping organizations and businesses understand disabled persons.

When Karen became Deputy Chief of Disabled Persons in the Illinois Attorney General's Office in 1985, she was given a lot of responsibility. She proved that she was a strong leader and fighter for people with disabilities. During the five years she was deputy chief, she helped write important state disability laws. Later, she became one of the leaders involved in the passage of a famous national law called "**ADA**," or Americans with Disabilities Act.

The ADA is important because it forbids discrimination against people with disabilities. It allows disabled people to receive the same services and opportunities as other people without disabilities. The law says that disabled people must have **access** to **employment**, transportation, education, health care, and housing. The ADA also is helping change the public's negative **attitudes** about disabled persons by educating and informing them. In 1990, the ADA became a law when President Bush signed it before Congress.

Karen Meyer showed up at WLS-TV in 1991 while doing a telethon. At the time she was executive director of the National Center for Access Unlimited. She worked with businesses across the United States to help inform them about ADA.

The manager of the TV station saw Karen, and he was very impressed because she was so **dynamic** and enthusiastic. He and the news director hired her to be a correspondent for their Eyewitness News on WLS-TV. Karen had no reporting experience before working at WLS-TV, but she learned fast, and her Monday night reports have become very popular in Chicago. Every week she reports on real-life stories. She explains, "I report about how different businesses and public places can make themselves accessible to disabled people."

In her stories, Karen appears live in the TV studio while she reads and signs from her script with closed-captions appearing on the TV. She **researches** and writes all of her own **scripts**. She also directs the camera crew and does interviews. "If I can make someone's life different, that's the success of my story," says Karen.

In 1994, Ms. Meyer was chosen by President Clinton to be vice chairperson of the President's Committee for Employment of People with Disabilities. Karen knows what it is like to be **discriminated** against because of her deafness. In 1977, she applied for a job at the City of Chicago's Office for Senior Citizens and Handicapped Persons. She was educated and qualified for the job, but she was not hired. The person who interviewed Karen turned her down. Karen says, "I didn't get the job because it required a lot of telephone work. Because I'm deaf, the interviewer thought I would not qualify."

Some people would give up, but Karen refused to feel sorry for herself. Two years later, she

went back to the same office and was interviewed by a different person who understood about disabled workers. Karen got the job and later became department supervisor! She says, "If I had one message to give employers, it would be to look at the person before them and see what they have to offer, not what is missing."

In 1992, Karen started her own company - a consulting **firm**. She continues to travel throughout the United States, speaking and counseling organizations and companies about the ADA and disability issues. She is also busy at WLS-TV doing her weekly show. When she is not working, Karen enjoys running, biking, cross-country skiing, and reading. She loves living in Chicago with her husband, Michael, and her two collies, Amos and Betty.

Check Your Understanding

1. How many Americans are disabled?

2. What are some disabilities that people can have?

3. What are some ways that a social worker can help people?

4. Can you list three different kinds of jobs Karen has had?

5. What happened to Karen when she interviewed for a job at the City of Chicago's Office for Senior Citizens and Handicapped Persons?

6. Why do you think Karen supports ADA (Americans with Disabilities Act)?

Write About

"Deaf people are capable," says Karen Meyer. Write a paragraph explaining why you think deaf people make good workers.

Paul Ogden:
Words to Know

commands	orders
companions	friends
to alert	to warn
CCI	Canine Companions for Independence. A special school in Santa Rosa, California, that trains signal dogs.
application	a written request
donations	gifts; contributions
to bond	to come together
secure	safe; protected
to respond	to answer; to react
to accompany	to go with
logo	a symbol; a design
flaw	a weakness; a fault

auditory skills	listening skills
support services	special help
	Example: notetakers, interpreters, counselors
valedictorian	a top honor student
currently	presently; now
legend	a famous person
discipline	training; control
to guarantee	to promise; to pledge
to excel	to be better or greater

Paul Ogden: Man's Best Friend

Part I

Would you pay $10,000 for a dog? Would you send your dog to school for over two years? Would you teach your dog over 50 **commands**? You would if you had a signal dog. What is a signal dog? Signal dogs are trained to alert and warn deaf owners to certain sounds they cannot hear; for example, doorbells, alarm clocks, and sirens. These special dogs are helpers and **companions**. Some people call them "hearing ear dogs," but Dr. Paul Ogden likes to use the term "signal dogs." He explains, "The dogs do not really hear for us; they signal or **alert** us to sounds."

In 1985, Paul lost his beloved eight-year-old dog, Lox. He had trained Lox since he was a puppy and they were great friends. When Lox became sick and died, Paul's wife, Anne, encouraged him to get another dog. She wrote to several different schools in the United States for signal dogs. Both Paul and Anne were impressed with a school called **CCI or Canine Companions for Independence**, located in Santa Rosa, California. They decided to find out more about CCI.

After reading lots of information and still longing for another dog, Paul and Anne applied for a signal dog at CCI. Canine Companions for Independence accepted their **application**. The Ogdens discovered that CCI trains their dogs for two years. It costs about $10,000 to do this, but money is given through **donations**. The Ogdens also found out that future owners had to attend a two-week training camp. The days are very long at the camp and sometimes difficult. Dogs and their owners spend 15 hours a day together, training and **bonding**.

At CCI trainers train dogs to help people with different needs. Signal dogs are important because they help deaf people become more independent and **secure**. Paul and Anne were hoping for a special dog, and soon they fell in love with a beautiful black Belgian sheepdog named Chelsea. Chelsea was smart and had a pleasant personality. She was able to learn and **respond** to 85 commands! The Ogdens had to learn all of these commands, too. Here are some commands signal dogs learn at CCI:

1. Dog's name—to get its attention
   (Note: Deaf people snap their fingers or say dog's name while snapping their fingers.)
2. "Let's go"—means the dog is to go with you on a walk.
3. "Go to bed"—used to send the dog to its own place.
4. "Wait"—used to tell the dog to wait for you in an area or a room.
5. "Come here"—calls the dog over to you.

Note: Deaf people could use either spoken commands or hand signs or both. Some of the hand signs were ASL (American Sign Language); some were not.

Dogs at CCI are trained to respond to many different sounds and noises. They respond to fire alarms, baby cries, microwave buzzers, and screams. Signal dogs that graduate from Canine Companions for Independence are called "working dogs." They are legally allowed to **accompany** their deaf owners everywhere, such as airports, restaurants, theatres, and department stores.

Chelsea goes everywhere with Paul and Anne. When they travel, Chelsea has her own special backpack with the CCI **logo**. Inside the pack is a water bowl and her traveling gear. The Ogdens feel proud of Chelsea. Paul says, "She is the perfect dog for us, but she has some **flaws**. She steals butter from the table and she loves to jump on our bed." Paul wrote a wonderful book about his experiences owning a signal dog, called *Chelsea: The Story of a Signal Dog.*

Photo by: G. Paul Bishop, Jr.

Part II

Dr. Paul Ogden was born in Staunton, Virginia. He says, "I've always been deaf, and if I could hear the noise would drive me crazy!" His mother and father raised four boys in a very happy home. Only Paul and his oldest brother were born deaf. Paul's parents decided to send him away to school. They chose a famous oral school in St. Louis, Missouri, called CID or Central Institute for the Deaf. Sign language was not allowed at CID, so Paul was encouraged to speak, lipread, and use his **auditory skills**. He stayed at CID for 10 years. Even though he returned home for holidays and summer vacation, he often got homesick for his family and pets.

46

"From my earliest days, dogs meant home to me in a special way," recalls Dr. Ogden. Since he spent most of his childhood away from home, Paul often thought about his family and pets. His favorite pet while growing up was a small reddish-brown dog that looked like a fox. His name was "Happy." When Happy died, Paul got other dogs. Then, when he went to college, he was too busy to take care of a pet. It was not until graduate school that Paul found Lox in a dog pound.

When Paul left CID, he attended Stonewall Jackson High School in West Virginia. He did not have an interpreter or other **support services**. Yet, in 1968 he graduated as the top honor student and **valedictorian** of his class. He admits his success came from hard work and the support he received from his family, friends, and teachers.

At the age of 19, Paul attended Antioch College in Ohio. He majored in math and computers. When he got the opportunity to study in England, he transferred to the University of Manchester for one year. Then he returned to Antioch to get his B.A. degree. He spent the next four years at the University of Illinois, and when he was 24 years old, he learned sign language.

Learning sign language opened up a new world for Paul. Along with signs, he became interested in psychology and teaching. He loved working with people and decided to become a college professor. After he got his M.A. and Ph.D. degrees at the University of Illinois, he moved to California and began his teaching career.

Paul **currently** lives in Fresno, California, with his lovely wife, Anne, and their dog, Chelsea. He is a professor of Deaf Education at California State University, Fresno. Dr. Ogden has received many awards and special honors. Recently, he was named the Outstanding Professor for 1995 at CSU, Fresno. Somehow he finds time to travel and write books, too.

Anne, who is hard-of-hearing, is a registered nurse, and she was honored as "Nurse of the Year—'95" at San Joaquin Valley Rehabilitation Hospital. Paul and Anne are **legends** in Fresno. They work hard and volunteer their time to help others. Dr. Paul Ogden says, "I have always told people hard work and **discipline** pay off in the long run. Having brains doesn't always **guarantee** success. It takes hard work and determination to **excel**."

Check Your Understanding

1. Why do you think some deaf people want to own a signal dog?

2. Why do you think it is so expensive to train a signal dog?

3. What are some sounds that signal dogs are trained to respond to?

4. How many commands does a signal dog learn at Canine Companions for Independence (CCI)?

5. Where do Paul and Anne Ogden live now?

6. How do you know that Chelsea is a smart dog?

Write About

Paul Ogden is a dog-lover. Write a paragraph telling about your favorite pet.

Learn More About It

Evelyn Glennie: The Impossible Dream

Evelyn Glennie, *Good Vibrations*.
Century Hutchinson, 1990.
Japan: Simul Press, 1992.
Arrow: paperback

Paul Ogden: Man's Best Friend

Paul Ogden, *Chelsea: The Story of a Signal Dog*.
Boston: Little, Brown & Co. 1992, hardbound.
New York: Fawcett Crest, 1993, softbound.

Paul Ogden, *The Silent Garden Revisted: Understanding Deaf Children*.
To be published fall, 1996.

Howie Seago: The Trailblazer

Howie Seago, *Visual Tales (Stories from the Attic)*.
Seattle: Sign a Vision.

Notes

Notes

Notes

Notes

Notes